Music for Double Bass & Piano

CONTENTS

To access audio, visit:
www.halleonard.com/mylibrary

Enter Code
7965-1192-3540-2270

ISBN 978-1-59615-626-5

Music Minus One

EXCLUSIVELY DISTRIBUTED BY

HAL•LEONARD®

7777 W. BLUEMOUND RD. P.O. BOX 13819 MILWAUKEE, WI 53213

Visit Hal Leonard Online at
www.halleonard.com

Contact us:
Hal Leonard
7777 West Bluemound Road
Milwaukee, WI 53213
Email: info@halleonard.com

In Europe, contact:
Hal Leonard Europe Limited
42 Wigmore Street
Marylebone, London, W1U 2RN
Email: info@halleonardeurope.com

In Australia, contact:
Hal Leonard Australia Pty. Ltd.
4 Lentara Court
Cheltenham, Victoria, 3192 Australia
Email: info@halleonard.com.au

PERFORMANCE GUIDE
COMMENTARY BY DAVID WALTER

WEINSTEIN
Contemporary Modal Solos

The Mixolydian is a very bright and happy piece which requires a light bow and staccato. The Hungarian emphasizes melody and legato. The last note in the Mixolydian presents a familiar problem: it is too long to be played in one bow. Practice the bow-change using the wrist as a 'shock-absorber' so that the smallest possible break is heard. It is also helpful to change at a rhythmic point where the piano chord will mask the change.

CAPUZZI
Concerto for Double Bass

This concerto, composed around 1800, still has a freshness and charm which makes it one of the bassist's alltime favorites. The first movement abounds in rhythmic interest: observe that each of the first five notes has a different time value; note the juxtaposition of triplets, sixteenths, eighths and dotted-eighths-and-sixteenths in the six measures before rehearsal number 3; note the alternation of staccato and legato dotted-eighths-and-sixteenths in the seventh measure of number 2. If these are all played faithfully, the movement will sparkle. Of course the second theme (at number 3) will be, in contrast, very smooth and legato in its first seven bars. The short cadenza was improvised at the time of the recording: this was the custom up until the nineteenth century and is good practice for the student. Using a few of the thematic phrases, in whole or in part, try your hand at constructing a cadenza utilizing every resource at your command: loud-soft. slow-fast, arco-pizzicato, arpeggios, scales, harmonics, ponticello, col legno — in other words, weave an extremely varied tapestry. You will enjoy it!

The second movement is a combination of sweet song and decorative accompaniment. The song (first 19 bars) should be warm and vibrant; the arpeggios and cross-string-16ths (at number 5) can be cool and subdued. This movement is truly a duet between you and the orchestra.

BOTTESINI
Reverie

Bottesini, the "Chopin" of double bass literature, was a celebrated composer and conductor (he conducted the premiere of "Aida" and composed a number of operas), but he is best remembered today as the virtuoso who enchanted European and American audiences with his superb bass-playing. This "Reverie" is typical in its use of rhythmic freedom, bitter-sweet harmonies, extreme upper register, harmonics, glissandos, the whole kit of romantic devices. It must be played very flexibly, with intense vibrato and extreme legato.

BOTTESINI
Concerto

Of the various concerti Bottesini composed, this first movement of his F♯ minor concerto, popularized in its present edition by Edouard Nanny, is the best known. It demands a powerful declamatory style in its opening theme; an extremely sweet and poignant legato, vibrato, and portamento in its second theme; and contains very "bravura" (flashy) scale and arpeggio passages. The cadenza must be free and very dramatic. This is a difficult movement: it is a gratifying commentary on the rapid rise in double bass performance standards that all advanced students now include this in their repertoire.

DRAGONETTI
Concerto

The most celebrated of double bassists, Dragonetti was a legend in his own time. He produced a substantial body of bass literature; recently the micro-filming of the music collection of the British Museum has brought to light (and, more recently, to publication) many of his works, including some ten concerti. This one, whose authenticity is still in doubt, is probably the most popular of all bass concertos. Its use of scales, arpeggios, harmonics, double-stops, legato and staccato passages presents the student and performer an opportunity to demonstrate all his technique and all his musicality. It is enormously helpful to memorize this movement so that your attention can be focussed on left-hand position and bow-placement. The bold high-register opening requires bowing very close to the bridge; your eyes can be very helpful in finding precisely the place on the string for maximum-intensity bowing. The harmonic passages may be slower and more tranquil with fine effect. Study the scales and arpeggios with great concentration so that you may finally produce very clean and tidy passage-work.

HINDEMITH
Sonata

This has become, in the 25 years since its composition, a classic in the bass repertoire. With it, Hindemith opened the door and invited composers to create new literature for the double bass. Hundreds of works have been written since then for the bass soloist, but this remains one of the most interesting and attractive. Note the variety of thematic ideas in the first movement: it starts gruff and forceful, continues in a romantic vein, utilizes harmonics most ingeniously, and tosses thematic fragments up and back in true duo-sonata style (rather than solo-and-accompaniment).

David Walter

Contemporary Modal Solos

Edited by Fred Zimmermann

MILTON WEINSTEIN

Mixolydian

Moderato (♩. = 60)

dim. poco a poco

Hungarian

Edited by Fred Zimmermann

MILTON WEINSTEIN

Concerto

Ist Movement

Edited by David Walter

ANTONIO CAPUZZI

5

+ = L. H. pizz.
* = Strike string hard with finger.

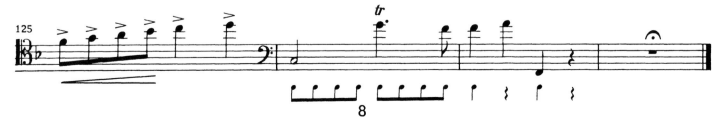

2nd Movement

Andante cantabile (♩ = 63)

9

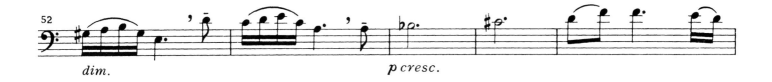

REVERIE

Edited by David Walter

GIOVANNI BOTTESINI

CONCERTO

Edited by David Walter

GIOVANNI BOTTESINI

CONCERTO in A

Edited by David Walter

DOMENICO DRAGONETTI

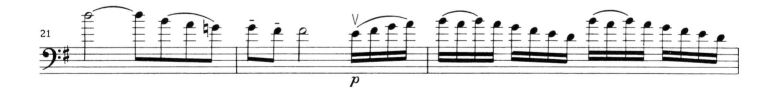

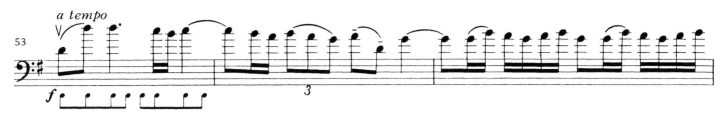

SONATA

Edited by David Walter

PAUL HINDEMITH

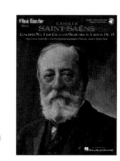

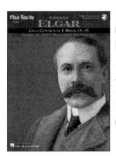

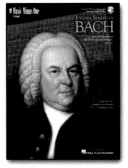